THE
NARNIA
TRIVIA BOOK

The Chronicles of Narnia®
by C. S. Lewis

Book One
The Magician's Nephew

Book Two
The Lion, the Witch and the Wardrobe

Book Three
The Horse and His Boy

Book Four
Prince Caspian

Book Five
The Voyage of the Dawn Treader

Book Six
The Silver Chair

Book Seven
The Last Battle

THE
NARNIA
TRIVIA BOOK

Inspired by *The Chronicles of Narnia*®
by C. S Lewis

With illustrations from *The Chronicles of Narnia*®
by Pauline Baynes

SCHOLASTIC INC.
New York Toronto London Auckland Sydney
Mexico City New Delhi Hong Kong

The Narnia Trivia Book
Copyright © 1999 by HarperCollins Publishers Inc.
Text and illustrations taken from the following Chronicles of Narnia books by C. S. Lewis: *The Magician's Nephew*, copyright © 1955 by C.S. Lewis Pte. Ltd. Copyright renewed 1983 by C.S. Lewis Pte. Ltd. *The Lion, the Witch and the Wardrobe*™, copyright © 1950 by C.S. Lewis Pte. Ltd. Copyright renewed 1978 by C.S. Lewis Pte. Ltd. *The Horse and His Boy*, copyright © 1954 by C.S. Lewis Pte. Ltd. Copyright renewed 1982 by C.S. Lewis Pte. Ltd. *Prince Caspian: The Return to Narnia*, copyright © 1951 by C.S. Lewis Pte. Ltd. Copyright renewed 1979 by C.S. Lewis Pte. Ltd. *The Voyage of the* Dawn Treader, copyright © 1952 by C.S. Lewis Pte. Ltd. Copyright renewed 1980 by C.S. Lewis Pte. Ltd. *The Silver Chair*, copyright © 1953 by C.S. Lewis Pte. Ltd. Copyright renewed 1981 by C.S. Lewis Pte. Ltd. *The Last Battle*, copyright © 1956 by C.S. Lewis Pte. Ltd. Copyright renewed 1984 by C.S. Lewis Pte. Ltd.

www.narnia.com

ISBN 978-0-06-267350-3

17 18 19 20 BR 10 9 8 7 6 5 4 3 2 1

The Magician's Nephew

1. What does Polly call the place where she plays on rainy days?

2. What is the first to travel into another world?

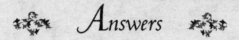

Answers

1. A smugglers' cave.

She had often drunk a quiet bottle of ginger-beer in there: the old bottles made it look more like a smugglers' cave.

2. A guinea-pig.

"I've tried it on a guinea-pig and it seemed to work. But then a guinea-pig can't tell you anything. And you can't explain to it how to come back."

The Magician's Nephew

3. What was in the box old Mrs. Lefay gave Uncle Andrew to destroy?

—

4. What colors are Uncle Andrew's rings?

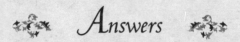 *Answers*

3. Dust from another world.

"Only dust," said Uncle Andrew. "Fine, dry dust. Nothing much to look at. Not much to show for a lifetime of toil, you might say."

4. Green and yellow.

The stuff in the yellow rings had the power of drawing you into the wood. . . . A green ring would take you out of the wood into a world.

The Magician's Nephew

5. What does Digory strike to wake Queen
   Jadis?

6. What is the name of Jadis's city?

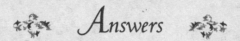

Answers

5. A bell.

He leaned forward, picked up the hammer, and struck the golden bell a light, smart tap.

6. Charn.

"Such was Charn, that great city, the city of the King of Kings, the wonder of the world, perhaps of all worlds."

The Magician's Nephew

7. What color is the sun in Charn?

8. What is Aunt Letty mending when Jadis arrives?

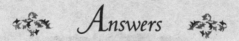 Answers

7. Red.

Low down and near the horizon hung a great, red sun, far bigger than our sun.

8. A mattress.

She was busily mending a mattress. It lay on the floor near the window and she was kneeling on it.

The Magician's Nephew

9. What does Uncle Andrew put on to make Jadis fall in love with him?

10. Where does Jadis stand to drive the hansom cab?

9. His best clothes.

He put on his best frock-coat, the one he kept for weddings and funerals. He got out his best tall hat and polished it up.

10. On the roof.

On the roof—not sitting, but standing on the roof—swaying with superb balance as it came at full speed round the corner with one wheel in the air—was Jadis the Queen of Queens and the Terror of Charn.

The Magician's Nephew

11. What does Aslan do to create Narnia?

12. Who is the first joke in Narnia?

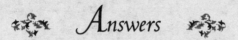

Answers

11. He sings.

And as he walked and sang the valley grew green with grass. It spread out from the Lion like a pool.

12. The jackdaw.

"Aslan! Aslan! Have I made the first joke? . . ."
   "No, little friend," said the Lion. "You have not made the first joke; you have only been the first joke."

The Magician's Nephew

13. What do the talking animals think Uncle
    Andrew is?

14. What do they do to him?

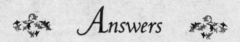 Answers

13. A tree.

"What do most of us think? Is it an animal or something of the tree kind?"

"Tree! Tree!" said a dozen voices.

14. They plant him.

"Very well," said the Elephant. "Then, if it's a tree it wants to be planted."

The Magician's Nephew

15. Who are the first King and Queen of Narnia?

16. What is Strawberry called once he becomes a flying horse?

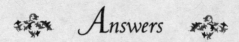

Answers

15. The cabby, Frank, and his wife, Helen.

"My children," said Aslan, fixing his eyes on both of them, "you are to be the first King and Queen of Narnia."

The Cabby opened his mouth in astonishment, and his wife turned very red.

16. Fledge.

"Be winged. Be the father of all flying horses," roared Aslan in a voice that shook the ground. "Your name is Fledge."

The Magician's Nephew

17. What does Digory bring home from Narnia?

18. Who eats an apple in order to get better?

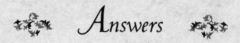

17. An apple.

The brightness of the Apple threw strange lights on the ceiling. Nothing else was worth looking at.

18. Digory's mother.

"Oh, darling, how lovely," said Digory's Mother.
"You will eat it, won't you? Please," said Digory.

The Lion, the Witch and the Wardrobe

1. How does Lucy leave the wardrobe door when she goes into it?

2. What is Mr. Tumnus holding when Lucy meets him at the lamppost?

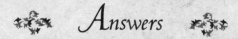

Answers

1. Open.

She had, of course, left the door open, for she knew that it is a very silly thing to shut oneself into a wardrobe.

2. An umbrella and some parcels.

One of his hands . . . held the umbrella: in the other arm he carried several brown-paper parcels.

The Lion, the Witch and the Wardrobe

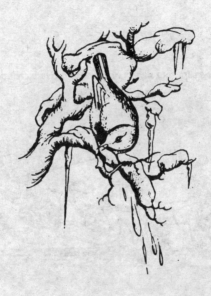

3. How many reindeer pull the White Witch's sledge?

4. Who guides the children to meet Mr. Beaver?

3. Two.

At last there swept into sight a sledge drawn by two reindeer.

4. A robin.

The Robin . . . kept going from tree to tree, always a few yards ahead of them, but always so near that they could easily follow it.

The Lion, the Witch and the Wardrobe

5. What does Mr. Beaver show the children to prove he is a friend?

6. What is Mrs. Beaver working at when the children first arrive?

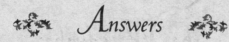

❦ *Answers* ❦

5. Lucy's handkerchief.

Lucy said, "Oh, of course. It's my handkerchief—the one I gave to poor Mr. Tumnus."

6. A sewing machine.

The first thing Lucy . . . saw was a kind-looking old she-beaver sitting in the corner with a thread in her mouth working busily at her sewing machine.

The Lion, the Witch and the Wardrobe

7. What does Edmund draw on the stone lion in the Witch's courtyard?

8. What does the Witch turn the party of squirrels, satyrs, a dwarf and a dog-fox into with her wand?

7. A moustache and a pair of spectacles.

He took a stump of lead pencil out of his pocket and scribbled a moustache on the lion's upper lip and then a pair of spectacles on its eyes.

8. Stone statues.

Instantly where the merry party had been there were only statues of creatures.

The Lion, the Witch and the Wardrobe

9. What causes the Witch's sledge to start skidding, jolting, and going slower?

10. Where do Peter, Susan, and Lucy meet Aslan?

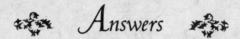
9. The thaw.

And soon Edmund noticed that the snow which splashed against them as they rushed through it was much wetter than it had been all last night.

10. At the Stone Table.

In the very middle of this open hilltop was the Stone Table.

The Lion, the Witch and the Wardrobe

11. What magic allows the Witch the right to kill Edmund?

12. Who nibbles away the ropes that bind Aslan?

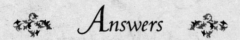

Answers

11. The Deep Magic.

"Well," said Aslan. "His offense was not against you."
  "Have you forgotten the Deep Magic?" asked the Witch.

12. Mice.

"I do believe—" said Susan. "But how queer! They're nibbling away at the cords!"
  "That's what I thought," said Lucy. "I think they're friendly mice."

The Lion, the Witch and the Wardrobe

13. What does Aslan do to bring the statues back to life?

14. What does Lucy give to Giant Rumblebuffin?

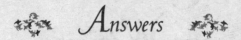 *Answers*

13. He breathes on them.

He had bounded up to the stone lion and breathed on him.

14. Her handkerchief.

"Yes, I have," said Lucy, standing on tip-toes and holding her handkerchief up as far as she could reach.

The Lion, the Witch and the Wardrobe

15. What does Edmund smash during the battle against the Witch's army?

16. Where are the four children crowned Kings and Queens of Narnia?

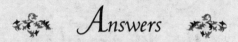 *Answers*

15. The Witch's wand.

"When he reached her he had sense to bring his sword smashing down on her wand instead of trying to go for her directly."

16. Cair Paravel.

And that night there was a great feast in Cair Paravel, and revelry and dancing, and gold flashed and wine flowed.

The Lion, the Witch and the Wardrobe

17. What are Peter, Susan, Edmund, and Lucy hunting when they see the lamppost again?

18. Who is the one person whom the children tell about their adventures in Narnia?

17. The white stag.

So these two Kings and two Queens . . . rode a-hunting with horns and hounds in the Western Woods to follow the White Stag.

18. Professor Kirke.

They felt they really must explain to the Professor why four of the coats out of his wardrobe were missing.

The Horse and His Boy

1. What was Shasta riding when he first arrived in Calormen?

2. What does Shasta fear to become if he stays with the Tarkaan?

1. A boat.

"And shortly after, the tide brought to the land a little boat in which there was nothing but a man lean with extreme hunger and thirst, . . . and an empty water-skin, and a child, still living."

2. A slave.

"But you'd better be lying dead tonight than go to be a human slave in his house tomorrow."
  "Then I'd better run away," said Shasta, turning very pale.

The Horse and His Boy

3. What is Bree's full name?

4. What is Aravis wearing when Shasta meets her?

❊❊ *Answers* ❊❊

3. Breehy-hinny-brinny-hoohy-hah.

"Breehy-hinny-brinny-hoohy-hah," said the Horse.
  "I'll never be able to say that," said Shasta. "Can I call you Bree?"

4. Her brother's armor.

"I arose and put on an armor of my brother's which I always kept in my chamber in his memory."

The Horse and His Boy

5. Who do the Narnians think Shasta is?

6. Who wants to marry Queen Susan?

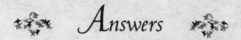

Answers

5. Prince Corin of Archenland.

"I'm being mistaken for a prince of Archenland, wherever that is. And these must be Narnians. I wonder where the real Corin is?"

6. Prince Rabadash of Calormen.

"Have you yet settled in your mind whether you will marry this dark-faced lover of yours, this Prince Rabadash, or no?"

The Horse and His Boy

7. How does Shasta leave the palace to
   escape from the Narnians?

8. Where does Shasta wait for Bree, Hwin,
   and Aravis?

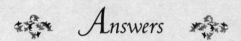

❧ Answers ❧

7. Through the window.

"How do I get away?"

"Look," said Corin. "Drop from this window onto the roof of the verandah."

8. The Tombs of the Ancient Kings.

There were about twelve Tombs, each with a low arched doorway that opened into absolute blackness.

The Horse and His Boy

9. Who recognizes Aravis in Tashbaan?

10. What do Aravis and Lasaraleen hide behind to avoid the Tisroc?

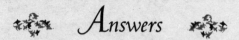

Answers

9. Lasaraleen.

She knew Lasaraleen quite well—almost as if they had been at school together—because they had often stayed in the same houses and been to the same parties.

10. A sofa.

They groped forward into the room and blundered into a sofa.

The Horse and His Boy

11. What is the ruler of Calormen called?

12. Whom is Aravis supposed to marry?

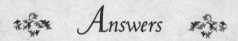

Answers

11. The Tisroc.

She immediately knew that he was the Tisroc. The least of the jewels with which he was covered was worth more than all the clothes and weapons of the Narnian lords put together.

12. Ahoshta Tarkaan.

Last of all came a little hump-backed, wizened old man in whom she recognized with a shudder the new Grand Vizier and her own betrothed husband, Ahoshta Tarkaan himself.

The Horse and His Boy

13. Who is the first person Shasta and Aravis meet in Archenland?

14. What two countries do the mountains divide?

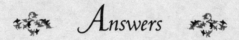

13. The Hermit of the Southern March.

"Are—are—are you," panted Shasta. "Are you King Lune of Archenland?"

The old man shook his head. "No," he replied in a quiet voice, "I am the Hermit of the Southern March."

14. Archenland and Narnia.

"Those are the big mountains between Archenland and Narnia. I was on the other side of them yesterday. I must have come through the pass in the night."

The Horse and His Boy

15. What does Shasta hurt during the battle?

16. Who is Shasta's father?

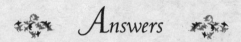 *Answers*

15. His knuckles.

Then a spear came straight at him and as he ducked to avoid it he rolled right off his horse, bashed his knuckles terribly against someone else's armor, and then—

16. King Lune.

"Apparently King Lune is my father," said Shasta. "I might really have guessed it."

The Horse and His Boy

17. Who is Shasta's brother?

18. What does Aslan turn Rabadash into as a punishment?

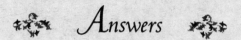

Answers

17. Prince Corin.

"Corin being so like me. We were twins, you see."

18. A donkey.

And he was standing on all fours, and his clothes disappeared, and everyone laughed louder and louder ... for now what had been Rabadash was, simply and unmistakably, a donkey.

Prince Caspian

1. Where are Lucy, Edmund, Susan, and
   Peter going when they are pulled into
   Narnia?

2. What does Susan find by the well in the
   ruins?

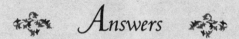

Answers

1. To school.

Here, in a few minutes, one train would arrive and take the girls away to one school, and in about half an hour another train would arrive and the boys would go off to another school.

2. A chess piece.

A little chess-knight, ordinary in size but extraordinarily heavy because it was made of pure gold; and the eyes in the horse's head were two tiny little rubies.

Prince Caspian

3. What are the ruins where the children
   have been staying?

4. Which of the children's old Christmas gifts
   is missing?

Answers

3. Cair Paravel.

"Have none of you guessed where we are?" said Peter. . . . "We are in the ruins of Cair Paravel itself."

4. Queen Susan's magic horn.

The bow was still there, and the ivory quiver, full of well-feathered arrows, but—"Oh, Susan," said Lucy. "Where's the horn?"

Prince Caspian

5. Whom did the Telmarine soldiers try to
   drown?

6. Who first told Caspian stories of Old
   Narnia?

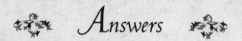

Answers

5. Trumpkin.

Peter now saw that it was really alive and was in fact a Dwarf, bound hand and foot but struggling as hard as he could.

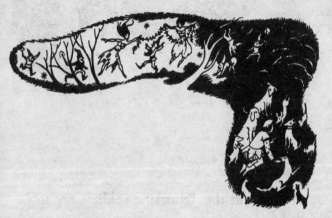

6. His nurse.

"Don't you know your Nurse was sent away for telling you about Old Narnia? The King doesn't like it."

Prince Caspian

7. What does Prince Caspian do when King Miraz's son is born?

~

8. What parting gift does Dr. Cornelius give Prince Caspian?

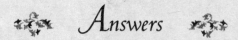

7. He flees for his life.

"Dear Prince, dear King Caspian, you must be very brave. You must go alone and at once."

8. Susan's magic horn.

"It is the magic horn of Queen Susan herself which she left behind her when she vanished from Narnia at the end of the Golden Age."

Prince Caspian

9. What is the first talking animal Prince Caspian meets?

10. Who betrays Prince Caspian to King Miraz?

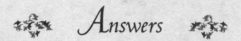

9. Trufflehunter the badger.

Caspian almost screamed with the shock as the sudden light revealed the face that was looking into his own. It was not a man's face, but a badger's.

10. Prince Caspian's horse, Destrier.

"The poor brute knew no better. When you were knocked off, of course, he went dawdling back to his stable in the castle."

Prince Caspian

11. What does Prince Caspian use to bring back the four Kings and Queens of Narnia?

12. What is Trumpkin's nickname?

11. Queen Susan's magic horn.

*"Great Scott!" said Peter. "So it was the horn—your own horn,
Su—that dragged us all off . . . the platform yesterday morning!"*

12. Our Dear Little Friend or our D.L.F.

"Need we go by the same way that Our Dear Little Friend came?"
  *"No more of that, your Majesty, if you love me," said the
Dwarf.*
  "Very well," said Edmund. "May I say our D.L.F.?"

Prince Caspian

13. Who sees Aslan first?

14. How does Aslan wake the tree people?

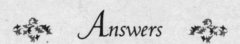

13. Lucy.

"The Lion," said Lucy. "Aslan himself. Didn't you see?" Her face had changed completely and her eyes shone.

14. He roars.

Aslan, who seemed larger than before, lifted his head, shook his mane, and roared.

Prince Caspian

15. Whom does Nikabrik want to bring back to defeat King Miraz?

⁓

16. Which lord kills King Miraz?

15. The White Witch.

"The Witch is dead. All the stories agree on that. What does Nikabrik mean by calling on the Witch?"

16. Glozelle.

But Glozelle stopped to stab his own King dead where he lay: "That's for your insult, this morning," he whispered as the blade went home.

Prince Caspian

17. What does Reepicheep lose in battle?

18. Where is the door the four children use to get back home?

Answers

17. His tail.

The fact was that he still had no tail—whether that Lucy had forgotten it or that her cordial, though it could heal wounds, could not make things grow again.

18. In the glade.

At one end of the glade Aslan had caused to be set up two stakes of wood, higher than a man's head and about three feet apart. A third, and lighter, piece of wood was bound across them at the top, uniting them, so that the whole thing looked like a doorway from nowhere into nowhere.

The Voyage of the Dawn Treader

1. What is Peter, Susan, Edmund, and Lucy's last name?

2. What do Eustace, Edmund, and Lucy use to get into Narnia?

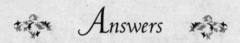

Answers

1. Pevensie.

Eustace Clarence disliked his cousins the four Pevensies, Peter, Susan, Edmund, and Lucy.

2. A painting.

Eustace jumped to try to pull it off the wall and found himself standing on the frame; in front of him was not glass but real sea, and wind and waves rushing up to the frame as they might to a rock.

The Voyage of the Dawn Treader

3. Whom does Caspian want to find on his quest on the *Dawn Treader*?

～

4. Why does Eustace need a dose of Lucy's magic cordial?

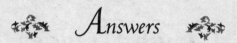

3. The seven lost lords of Narnia.

"I swore an oath that, if once I established peace in Narnia, I would sail east myself for a year and a day to find my father's friends or to learn of their deaths and avenge them if I could."

4. He's seasick.

But he took a drop from her flask, and though he said it was beastly stuff ... it is certain that his face came the right color a few moments after he had swallowed it.

The Voyage of the Dawn Treader

5. Whom does Eustace swing around by the tail?

---

6. Who captures Caspian, Lucy, Edmund, and Eustace on the Lone Islands?

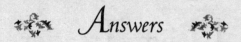

5. Reepicheep.

*Anyway, as soon as he saw that long tail hanging down …
he thought it would be delightful to catch hold of it, swing
Reepicheep round by it once or twice upside-down, then run
away and laugh.*

6. Pug and his slave traders.

*"So that's what you are," said Caspian. "A kidnapper and slaver.
I hope you're proud of it."*

The Voyage of the
Dawn Treader

7. What does Eustace try to steal after the storm?

8. What does the *Dawn Treader* lose in the storm?

Answers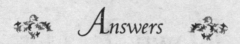

7. Water.

"And then Caspian showed up in his true colors as a brutal tyrant and said out loud for everyone to hear that anyone found 'stealing' water in future would 'get two dozen.'"

8. Her mast.

"The night we lost our mast (there's only a stump left now), . . . they forced me to come on deck and work like a slave."

The Voyage of the Dawn Treader

9. What does Eustace become after he puts on the bracelet from the dragon's treasure?

⁓

10. What is the Dufflepuds' problem?

9. A dragon.

He had turned into a dragon while he was asleep. Sleeping on a dragon's hoard with greedy, dragonish thoughts in his heart, he had become a dragon himself.

10. They're invisible.

"In the end we see a spell for making people invisible. And we thought we'd rather be invisible than go on being as ugly as all that."

The Voyage of the
Dawn Treader

11. What is the only direction the pages of
the magic book turn?

12. How many legs do the Dufflepuds have?

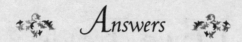

Answers

11. Forward.

You couldn't turn back. The right-hand pages, the ones ahead, could be turned; the left-hand pages could not.

12. One.

Each body had a single thick leg right under it (not to one side like the leg of a one-legged man) and at the end of it, a single enormous foot.

The Voyage of the Dawn Treader

13. What do the Dufflepuds use as boats?

14. What comes true on the dark island?

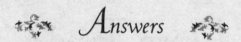

Answers

13. Their feet.

The huge single foot of a Monopod acted as a natural raft or boat, and when Reepicheep had taught them how to cut rude paddles for themselves, they all paddled about the bay and round the Dawn Treader.

14. Dreams.

For it had taken everyone just that half-minute to remember certain dreams they had had—dreams that make you afraid of going to sleep again—and to realize what it would mean to land on a country where dreams come true.

The Voyage of the
Dawn Treader

15. Which people were once stars?

16. Whom does Lucy see underwater near the End of the World?

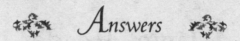 *Answers*

15. Coriakin and Ramandu.

"I am a star at rest, my daughter," answered Ramandu. "When I set for the last time, decrepit and old beyond all that you can reckon, I was carried to this island."

16. Sea People.

And all the Sea People were sitting on their horses staring up at what had happened. They seemed to be talking and laughing.

The Voyage of the Dawn Treader

17. How does the water taste near the End of the World?

⌣

18. What covers the surface of the water near the End of the World?

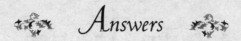 # Answers

17. Sweet.

"I tell you the water's sweet," said the Mouse. "Sweet, fresh. It isn't salt."

18. Lilies.

Whiteness, shot with the faintest color of gold, spread round them on every side, except just astern where their passage had thrust the lilies apart and left an open lane of water that shone like dark green glass.

The Silver Chair

1. What is the name of Jill and Eustace's school?

2. What happens when Eustace tries to save Jill on the cliff?

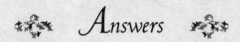 *A*nswers

1. Experiment House.

Jill looked round and saw the dull autumn sky and heard the drip off the leaves and thought of all the hopelessness of Experiment House.

2. He falls off.

At the same moment, Scrubb himself, with a terrified scream, had lost his balance and gone hurtling to the depths.

The Silver Chair

3. Who blows Jill and Eustace to Narnia?

4. Who is the old man Jill and Eustace see getting on the ship?

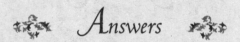

Answers

3. Aslan.

Floating on the breath of the Lion was so extremely comfortable. She found she could lie on her back or on her face and twist any way she pleased.

4. King Caspian.

"What is the King's name?" asked Eustace.
"Caspian the Tenth," said the Owl.

The Silver Chair

5. What does Jill ride when she leaves the castle?

6. What killed Prince Rilian's mother?

5. An Owl.

The Owl stood on the window-sill with his back to the room and raised his wings. Jill had to climb onto his short fat body and get her knees under the wings and grip tight.

6. A serpent.

A great serpent came out of the thick wood and stung the Queen in her hand. All heard her cry out and rushed toward her, and Rilian was first at her side.

The Silver Chair

7. What sort of creature is Puddleglum?

8. What game are the giants playing when Eustace, Jill, and Puddleglum see them?

Answers

7. A Marsh-wiggle.

"Where on earth are we?" asked Jill.
"In the wigwam of a Marsh-wiggle," said Eustace.

8. Cock-shies.

"They play cock-shies most fine mornings. About the only game they're clever enough to understand."

The Silver Chair

9. For what celebration do Jill, Eustace, and Puddleglum go to the giants?

---

10. What is the name of the giants' house?

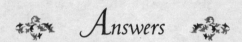

Answers

9. The Autumn Feast.

"Only tell them," answered the Lady, *"that She of the Green Kirtle salutes them by you, and has sent them two fair Southern children for the Autumn Feast."*

10. Harfang.

The only things she thought about were her cold hands (and nose and chin and ears) and hot baths and beds at Harfang.

The Silver Chair

11. What do the letters in the ruined city say?

12. Whom are the giants planning to eat at the Autumn Feast?

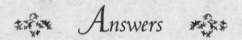

Answers

11. UNDER ME.

To crown all, in large, dark lettering across the center of the pavement, ran the words UNDER ME.

12. Eustace, Jill, and Puddleglum.

"It's a cookery book," thought Jill without much interest. . . . It ran—

MAN. *This elegant little biped has long been valued as a delicacy. It forms a traditional part of the Autumn Feast, and is served between the fish and the joint.*

The Silver Chair

13. Who is the black knight?

~~~

14. How long was Prince Rilian enchanted in the Underworld?

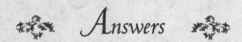

Answers

13. Prince Rilian.

"You may well believe that I know Narnia, for I am Rilian, Prince of Narnia, and Caspian the great King is my father."

14. Ten years.

"How long then have I been in the power of the witch?"
  "It is more than ten years since your Highness was lost in the woods at the north side of Narnia."

15. What does the Queen of Underland become when she attacks Prince Rilian?

16. Where are the gnomes in Underland from?

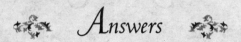
15. A serpent.

The great serpent which the Witch had become, green as poison, thick as Jill's waist, had flung two or three coils of its loathsome body round the Prince's legs.

16. Bism.

"You see, we're all poor gnomes from Bism whom the Witch has called up here by magic to work for her."

The Silver Chair

17. What celebration does Jill interrupt when she comes out of the earth?

18. What must King Caspian do before visiting Eustace and Jill's world?

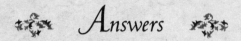

17. The Great Snow Dance.

This is called the Great Snow Dance and is done every year in Narnia on the first moonlit night when there is snow on the ground.

18. Die.

"Sir," said Caspian, "I've always wanted to have just one glimpse of their world. Is that wrong?"

"You cannot want wrong things any more, now that you have died, my son," said Aslan.

The Last Battle

1. What does Puzzle fish out of Caldron Pool?

---

2. What does Shift make with it?

✣ Answers ✣

1. A lion skin.

The Ape was too busy going round and round the Thing and spreading it out and patting it and smelling it. Then a wicked gleam came into his eye and he said:

"It is a lion's skin."

2. A coat.

"Come and try on your beautiful new lion-skin coat," said Shift.

The Last Battle

3. Who does Shift pretend Puzzle is?

4. Who kills the Calormenes who are forcing the Talking Narnian Horses to work?

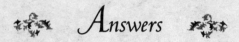

Answers

3. Aslan.

"If anyone saw you now, they'd think you were Aslan, the Great Lion, himself."

4. Tirian and Jewel.

When Tirian knew that the Horse was one of his own Narnians, there came over him and over Jewel such a rage that they did not know what they were doing. The King's sword went up, the Unicorn's horn went down. They rushed forward together.

The Last Battle

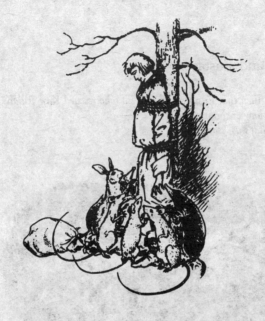

5. Who unties King Tirian from the tree?

———

6. How do Jill, Eustace, and Tirian disguise themselves?

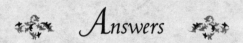

5. Jill and Eustace.

"Are you then that Eustace and that Jill who rescued King Rilian from his long enchantment?"
    "Yes, that's us," said Jill.

6. As Calormenes.

"And look on this stone bottle. In this there is a juice which, when we have rubbed it on our hands and faces, will make us brown as Calormenes."

The Last Battle

7. Whom does Jill steal from the stable?

8. Which dwarf joins King Tirian, Eustace, and Jill?

Answers

7. Puzzle.

"He was very fed up with the stable and quite ready to come—weren't you, Puzzle dear?"

8. Poggin.

"Who goes there!" shouted the King.

"Only me, Sire," came a voice. "Me, Poggin the Dwarf. I've only just managed to get away from the others. I'm on your side, Sire: and on Aslan's."

The Last Battle

9. What creature has a bird's head, a man's shape, and four arms?

＿

10. Who tells King Tirian about the invasion of Narnia?

9. Tash.

"He took me into the great temple of Tash. There I saw it, carved above the altar."
  "Then that—that thing—was Tash?" said Eustace.

10. Farsight the Eagle.

He alighted on a rocky crag a few feet from Tirian, bowed his crested head, and said in his strange eagle's-voice, "Hail, King."
  "Hail, Farsight," said Tirian.

The Last Battle

11. What weapons does Jill use during the battle?

---

12. Whom does Tirian meet in the stable?

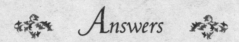
11. A bow and arrows.

Then he heard twang-and-zipp on his left and one Calormene fell: then twang-and-zipp again and the Satyr was down. "Oh, well done, daughter!" came Tirian's voice; and then the enemy were upon them.

12. The seven Kings and Queens.

And Tirian turned to see who had spoken....
   Seven Kings and Queens stood before him, all with crowns on their heads and all in glittering clothes.

The Last Battle

13. Of Lucy, Edmund, Susan, and Peter, who has not come back to Narnia?

14. What falls from the sky of Narnia?

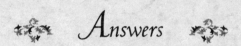

Answers

13. Susan.

"Has not your Majesty two sisters? Where is Queen Susan?"
"My sister Susan," answered Peter shortly and gravely, "is no longer a friend of Narnia."

14. The stars.

But stars in that world are not the great flaming globes they are in ours. They are people.... So now they found showers of glittering people, all with long hair like burning silver and spears like white-hot metal, rushing down to them out of the black air, swifter than falling stones.

The Last Battle

15. What covers the land after the stars fall and the trees and grass disappear?

16. Who greets the Narnians at the gate of the walled garden?

Answers

15. The sea.

And now they could see what it was that was coming. . . . It was a foaming wall of water. The sea was rising.

16. Reepicheep.

Tirian breathed fast with the sheer wonder of it, for now he knew that he was looking at one of the great heroes of Narnia, Reepicheep the Mouse.